PENELOPE POLARS™

POLARS

PLASTIC JOURNEY

To my children Isobel & Jack.

Even the smallest person can
make a world of difference.
We are on this journey together
for a brighter future.
X

With special thanks to Holly Shackleton.
Eternally grateful for all your help.

Written By Clare Beckett
Illustration and Design: Richie Evans

Published in association with Bear With Us Productions

PENELOPE POLARS™

PLASTIC JOURNEY

Written By Clare Beckett

Illustrated By Richie Evans

BEAR WITH US PRODUCTIONS

Penelope Polar is a little white bear, she loves her home and she treats it with care.

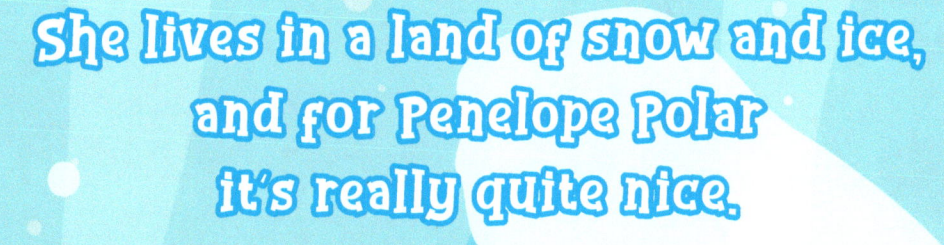

She lives in a land of snow and ice,
and for Penelope Polar
it's really quite nice.

She goes for a walk down by the sea,
then for a swim to catch fish for her tea

One day, Penelope saw something new.
It was hard, it was plastic and
there were more than a few.

Each day that she walked she saw more and more, until one day it got stuck on her paw.

Penelope Polar grew very sad.
She loved her home
but it was getting quite bad.

She went to bed with
a great big yawn,
and decided to leave
when it was dawn.

As she travelled she learnt more about plastic;
if people recycled that would be fantastic.

Onwards she walked into cities and towns
but all of the faces turned into frowns.

People started to stop and stare -
Penelope Polar didn't belong there.

Everywhere Penelope walked,
more and more people talked and talked.

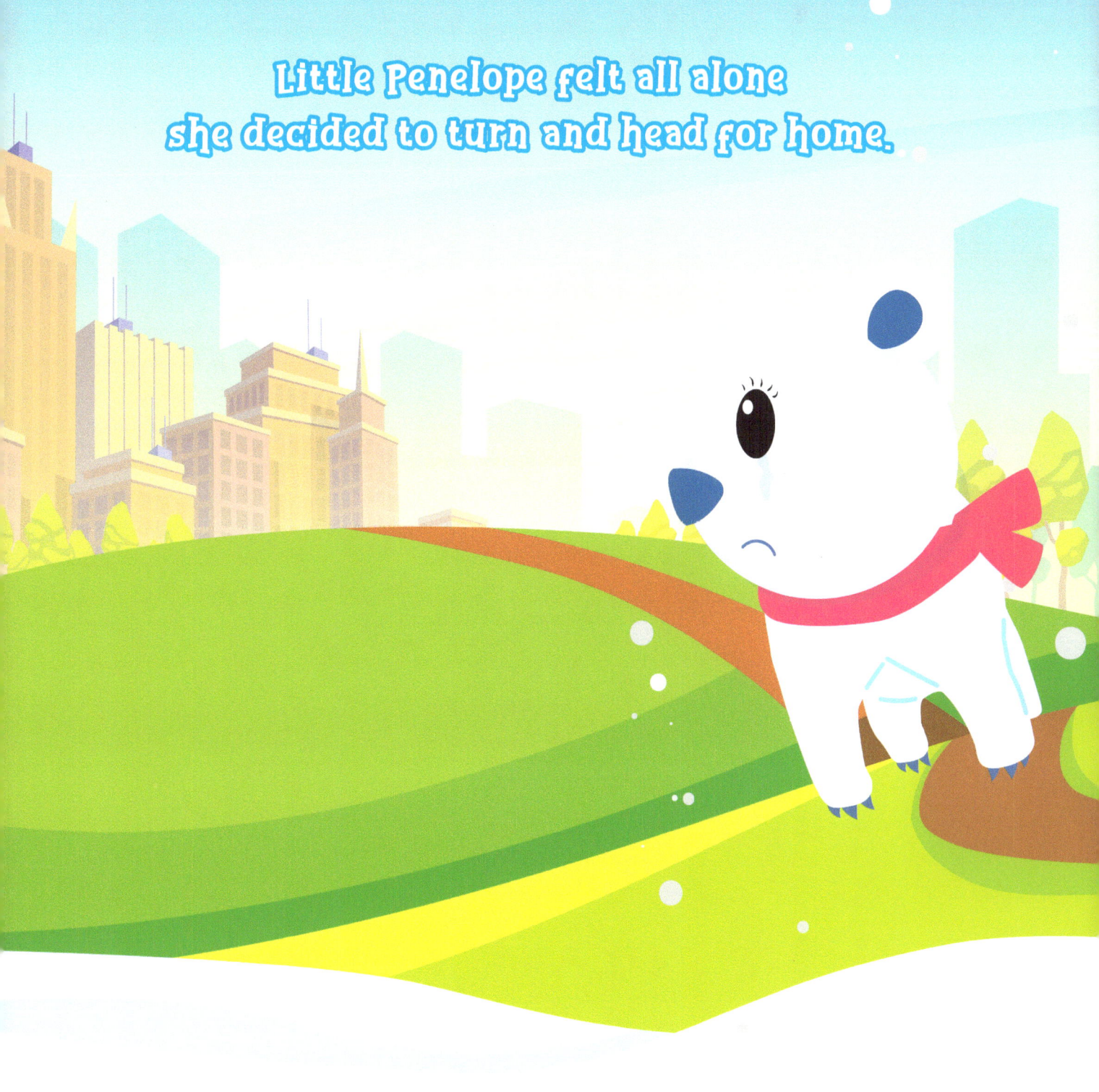

Little Penelope felt all alone
she decided to turn and head for home.

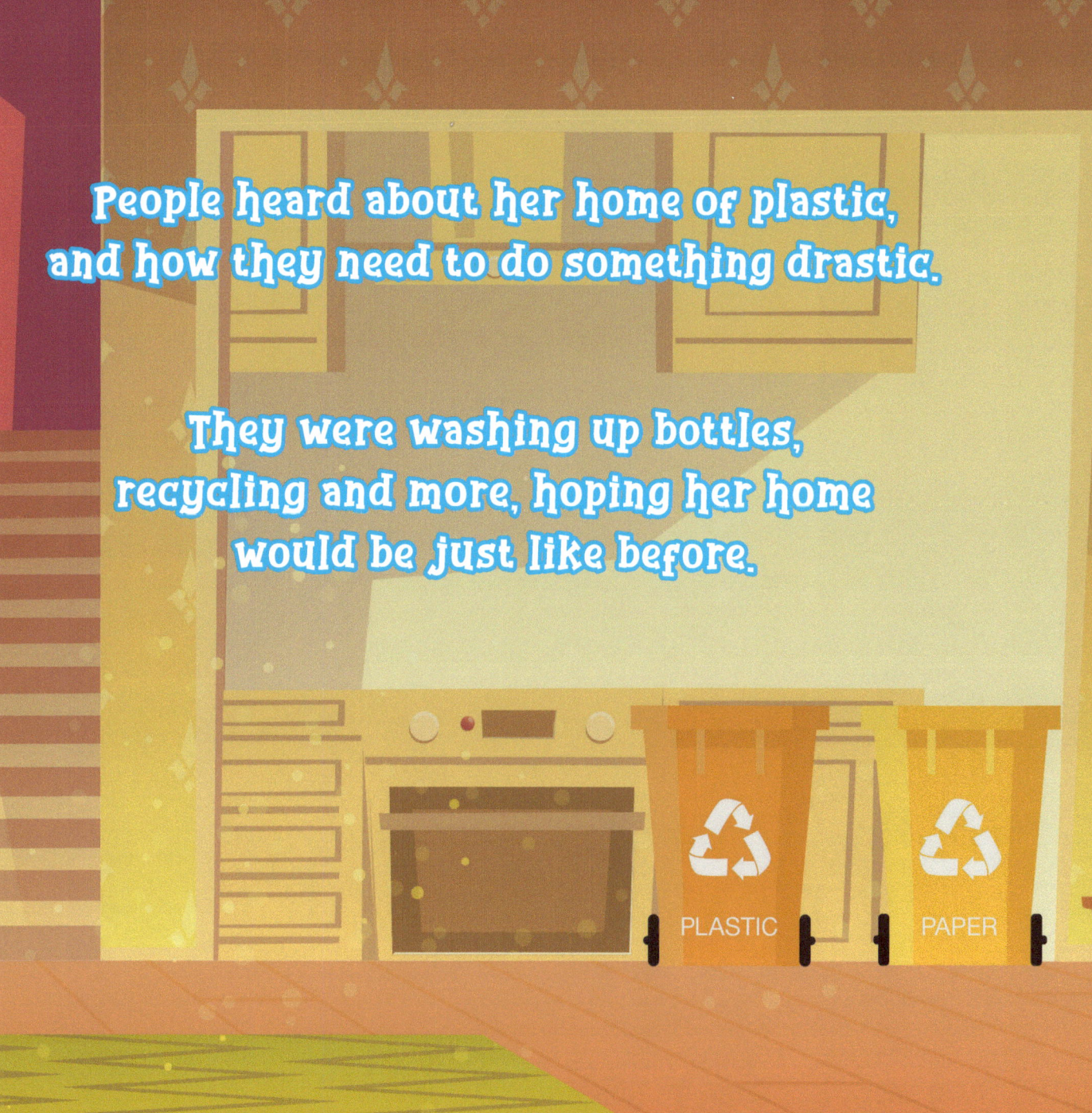

People heard about her home of plastic,
and how they need to do something drastic.

They were washing up bottles,
recycling and more, hoping her home
would be just like before.

PLASTIC

PAPER

As Penelope continued to roam
she could feel the cold
and felt closer to home.

But as Penelope began to get near she could
see lots of people starting to cheer!

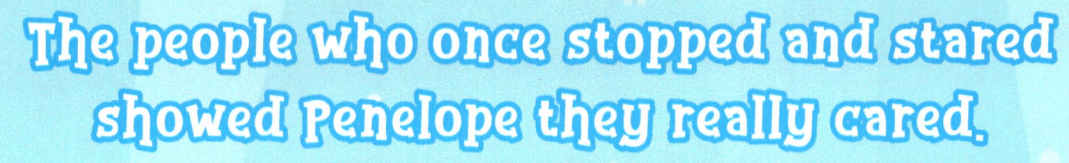

The people who once stopped and stared
showed Penelope they really cared.

She felt the snow beneath her paw;
it wasn't plastic like before.
They'd picked up the plastic from the snow
and told Penelope they had more to show

They'd cleared the plastic from the sea,
so now she could catch a fish for tea.

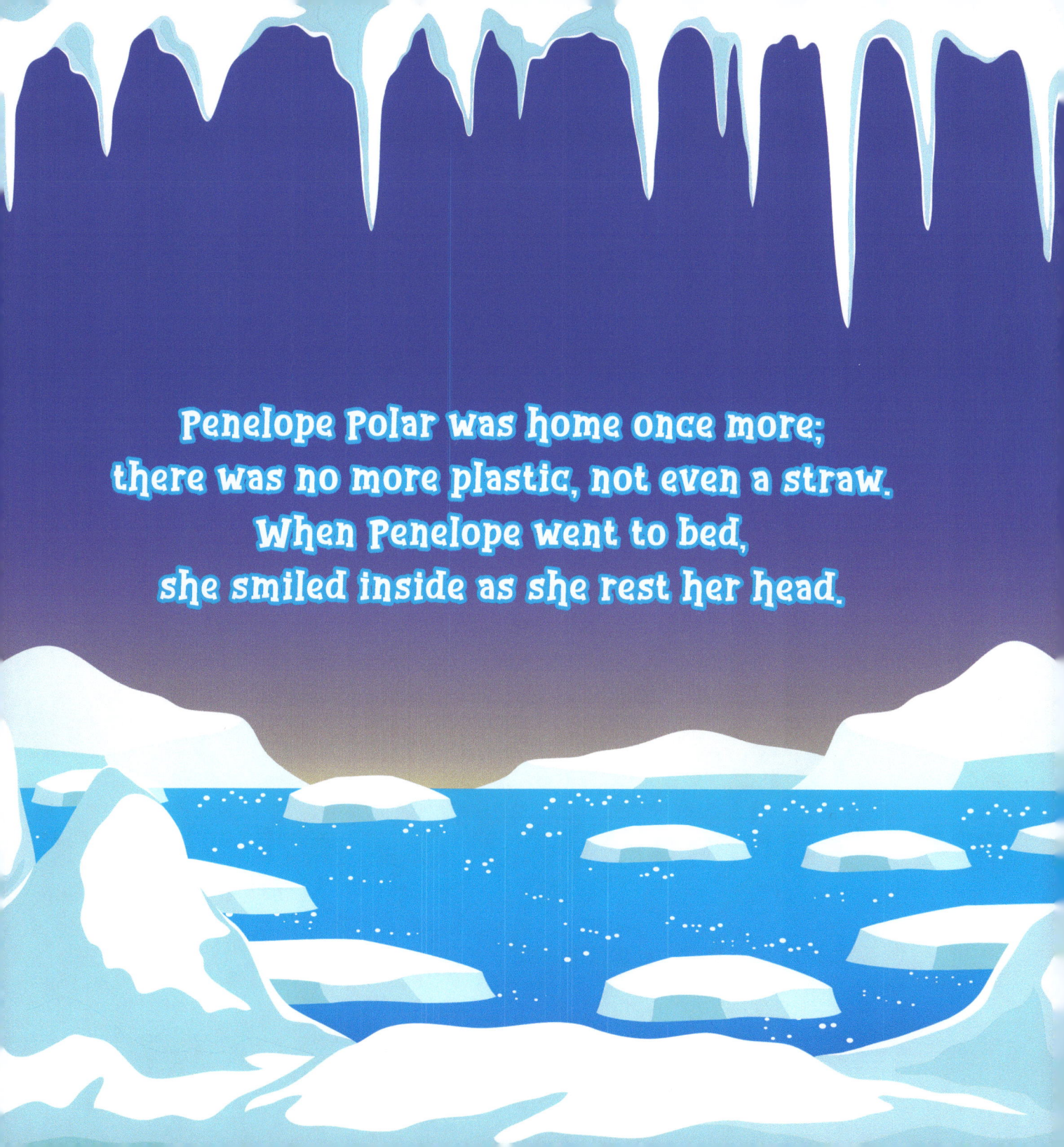

Penelope Polar was home once more;
there was no more plastic, not even a straw.
When Penelope went to bed,
she smiled inside as she rest her head.

With a little time
and care,

you can help
the polar bear.

THE END

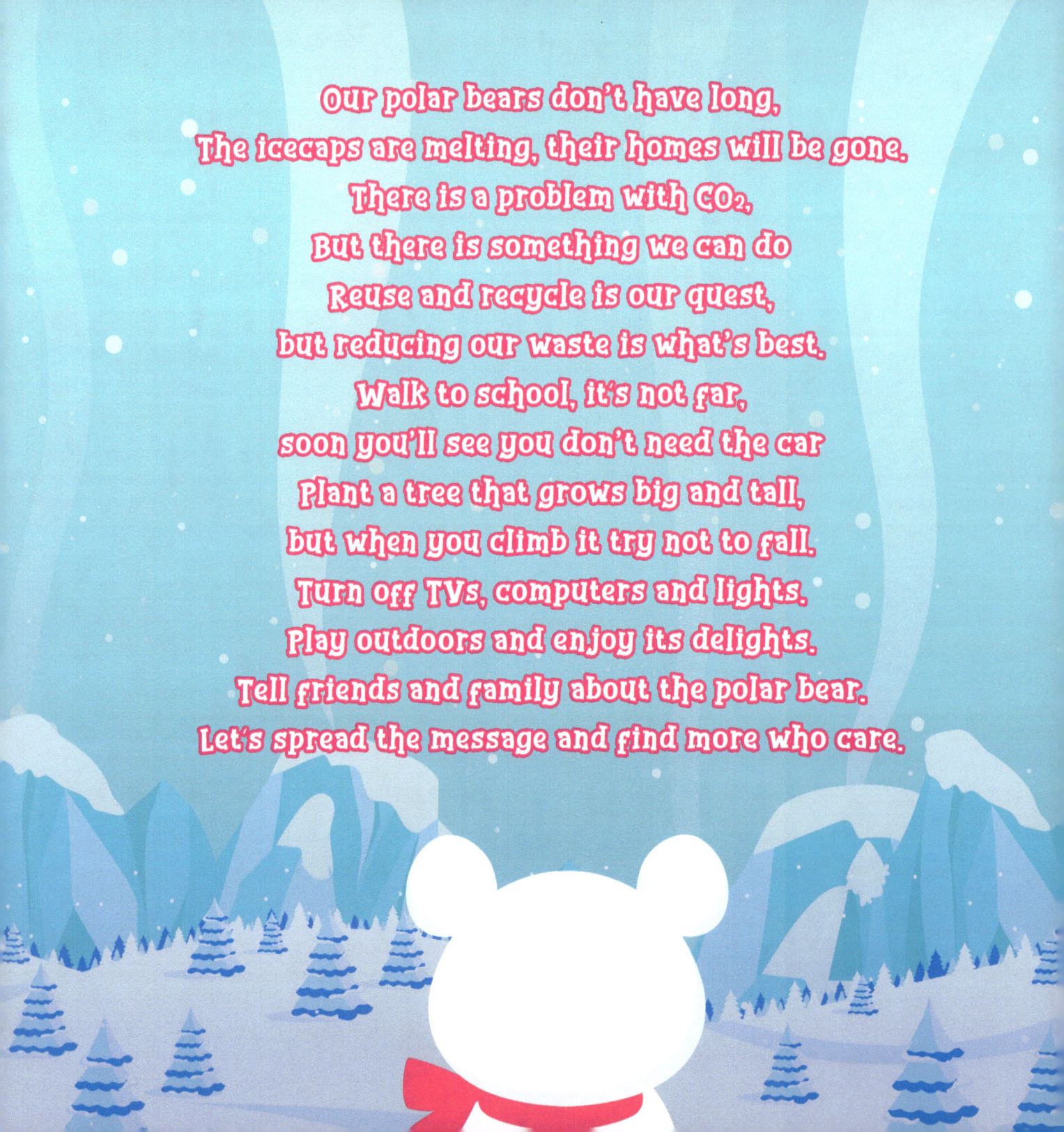

Our polar bears don't have long,
The icecaps are melting, their homes will be gone.
There is a problem with CO_2,
But there is something we can do
Reuse and recycle is our quest,
but reducing our waste is what's best.
Walk to school, it's not far,
soon you'll see you don't need the car
Plant a tree that grows big and tall,
but when you climb it try not to fall.
Turn off TVs, computers and lights.
Play outdoors and enjoy its delights.
Tell friends and family about the polar bear.
Let's spread the message and find more who care.

Help Penelope with the Recycling

1.

2.

3.

4.

5.

PLASTIC

A

PAPER

B

ORGANIC

C

GLASS

D

METAL

E

There are some incredible charities working hard to fight plastic pollution and preserve our planet.

Friends of the Earth and Sea Shepherd UK are two charities who have been working hard to make a change.

To learn more about their campaigns and support them in their quest please visit their websites for more details

www.seashepherd.org

www.friendsoftheearth.UK

PROUDLY SUPPORTING
SEA SHEPHERD

www.ingramcontent.com/pod-product-compliance
Lightning Source LLC
Chambersburg PA
CBHW060809290526
45792CB00005BA/1586

9781089535638